G000154882

Friendship

Many people will walk in and out of your life,
but only true *friends*
will leave footprints in your heart.

[ELEANOR ROOSEVELT]

M·I·L·K™

MOMENTS INTIMACY LAUGHTER KINSHIP

FRIENDSHIP
Copyright © 2004 PQ Publishers Limited. Published under license from
M.I.L.K. Licensing Limited.
www.milkphotos.com

All copyrights of the photographic images are owned by the individual
photographers who have granted M.I.L.K. Licensing Limited the exclusive
license to use them.

This edition published in 2004 by WPL, The Perfume Factory,
140 Wales Farm Road, London W3 6UG.
www.wpl.eu.com

Edited and designed by WPL
Printed in China

ISBN 1-904264-34-4

All rights reserved. No part of this publication may be reproduced (except
brief passages for the purpose of review), stored in a retrieval system or
transmitted in any form by any means, electronic, mechanical, photocopying,
recording or otherwise, without the prior written permission of the publisher.

Inspired by the 1950s landmark photographic exhibition,
"The Family of Man", M.I.L.K. began as an epic global search to
develop a collection of extraordinary and geographically diverse
images portraying humanity's Moments of Intimacy, Laughter and
Kinship (M.I.L.K.). This search took the form of a photographic
competition – probably the biggest and almost certainly the most
ambitious of its kind ever to be conducted. Chosen from 40,000
entries worldwide, the 300 winning images cut across race and
nationality and celebrate what it is to be part of a family, to share
the gift of friendship and more than anything else, to be loved.

These photographs were first published as three books entitled
"Family", "Friendship" and "Love" in early 2001 and are now
featured in a range of products worldwide,
in nine different languages in more than 20 countries.
M.I.L.K. is also a travelling exhibition.

True **friends** are a sure refuge.

[ARISTOTLE]

Great friends are hard to find,

difficult to leave

and impossible to forget.

In the sweetness of friendship let there be
laughter and sharing of pleasures.

[KAHLIL GIBRAN]

I am surrounded by angels

but I call them my best friends.

With a good friend you can
dance your cares away.

Laughter is the shortest distance between two people.

[VICTOR BORGE]

A faithful friend is the medicine of life.

When being together

is more important than what you do,

you are a true friend.

Real **friends** are those who, when you've made a fool of yourself, don't feel that you've done a permanent job.

[ERWIN T. RANDALL]

A friend is, as it were, a second self.

[CICERO]

Wherever you are

  it is your friends

who make your world.

[WILLIAM JAMES]

One loyal friend is worth

ten thousand relatives.

[EURIPIDES]

Friendship is one mind in two bodies.

It is so easy to smile

in the company of friends.

To have *joy* one must share it.

[LORD BYRON]

Nothing is more precious than a true friend.

No road is long with good company.

[TURKISH PROVERB]

Friendship is a sheltering tree.

[COLERIDGE]

Hold a true friend
with both your hands.

[NIGERIAN PROVERB]

Side by side or miles apart,

dear friends are always close
to the heart.

Where there is friendship
there is happiness.

With true friends we can be ourselves.

The most wasted day of all

is that on which

we have not laughed.

[SEBASTINE CHAMFORT]

Don't walk in front of me, I may not follow;

Don't walk behind me, I may not lead;

Walk beside me and
just be my friend.

[ALBERT CAMUS]

M.I.L.K. IMAGES

Two elderly ladies cheer on a friend as she plays
'Hopscotch' in San Rafael, California, USA.
© Charles Cormany / photolibrary.com

Bonnie's enthusiastic greeting is matched by a delighted
smile from friend Nancy in Washington DC, USA.
© Noelle Tan

Smiles of encouragement – six-year-old dancers Natasha
and Mitalee look to each other for confidence before
performing in front of a capacity crowd at the Houston
International Festival, Texas, USA.
© Janice Rubin

Taking cover – three young friends share the shelter of
an umbrella as they wait patiently for an open-air rock
concert to begin in London, England.
© Andreas Heumann

Two Mayan children share laughter and cuddles in Panajachel, Guatemala.
© David Tak-Wai Leung

Musicians and old friends Ruben and Ibrahin celebrate the release of their new CD at a café in Madrid, Spain.
© Cristina Piza

Free fall – four bikini-clad friends leap off a pier into the water below in Miami, Florida, USA.
© K Hatt

Dancing Partners – as two-year-old toddlers Harry and Margaret take to the floor in New York, USA, they can't resist giving each other a hug.
© Darien Mejía-Olivares

Two elderly friends share a joke as they go about their daily work in Chiang Rai, Thailand. They are drying native grass to be made into brooms.
© Pisit Senanunsakul

A boy's best friend – nine-year-old Jonathan prepares to take the plunge at his favourite swimming spot in Auckland, New Zealand. His dog Harry won't be far behind.
© Terry Winn

Sisters Dorothy and Annie, both over 90, enjoy a quiet moment together. They have taken a seat opposite a country church to watch a wedding party in Owthorpe, in Nottinghamshire, England.
© Steve Hotson

Christmas in Singapore – as the photographer gets his shop window ready for the festive season, his cheeky young relatives do their best to distract him.
© Bernard Poh Lye Kiat

Graceful under a heavy load – two Indian women walk side by side as they carry vegetables to market in Calcutta, India.
© Thomas Patrick Kiernan

Friendship means playing on the same side – a young soccer team in Belfast, Northern Ireland.
© Lance Jones

A retired Canadian war veteran shares a pensive moment with a close companion near Ottawa, Ontario, Canada. Home is an old school bus, which he shares with 15 energetic dogs.
© John A. Hryniuk

In the bright sunshine of Miami, Florida, USA, two friends make sure their noses are well protected as they stroll arm in arm along South Beach.
© Gay Block

The faces of six young friends as they take a break from lessons at their school in Phan Rang city, Vietnam.
© Thanh Long

Taste testing in Averill Park, in New York state, USA – five-year-old Abigail is curious to see whether Samantha's lollipop has a different flavour from her own.
© Linda Heim

Close companions – William Bossidy listens attentively to his friend John Noonan, a fellow resident at their nursing home in Florida, USA.
© Marianne Thomas

As his friends stride out along a dusty village street near Tijuana, Mexico, a young boy – and his trousers – try to keep up.
© Michael Chiabaudo

Conversation comes easily to two old friends as they relax opposite the Shiv Temple of Bilawali in Dewas, India.
© Kailash Soni

Open air entertainment – two children are happy to amuse themselves during the interval of an outdoor music concert in Linköping, Sweden.
© Tetsuaki Oda

An inseparable pair – elderly Ukrainian sisters caught on film during a visit to Cleveland, Ohio, USA.
© Bernard Mendoza

In Rumah Bilar in Sibu, Malaysia, young friends spend an evening making their own fun by the riverside.
© King Tuang Wong

Two kilted friends stand out from the crowd at the Gay Pride Festival in London, England.
© Davy Jones

An English tradition — deckchairs on the pier provide a typical holiday setting for three friends taking a break in Brighton, in the south of England.
© David Williams

A country lane in Olympia, Washington, USA, becomes an adventurous path for childhood friends Keegan, aged six, and Graeme, seven.
© Pat Justis